Anything You Ca 2
Doin' What Come 26
The Girl That I Marry 30
I Got Lost in His Arms 46
I Got the Sun in the Morning 14
I'll Share It All with You 42
Moonshine Lullaby 23
My Defenses Are Down 10
An Old Fashioned Wedding 36
There's No Business Like Show Business 18
They Say It's Wonderful 33
You Can't Get a Man with a Gun 6

Applications for performance of this work, whether legitimate, stock, amateur or foreign, should be addressed to:
THE RODGERS & HAMMERSTEIN THEATRE LIBRARY
229 West 28th Street, 11th Floor • New York, NY 10001
Phone: (212) 564-4000 Fax: (212) 268-1245
E-mail: theatre@rnh.com Website: www.rnh.com

ISBN 0-7935-0855-X

Irving Berlin Music Company®
www.irvingberlin.com

Exclusively Distributed By

7777 W. Bluemound Rd. P.O. Box 13819 Milwaukee, WI 53213

Anything You Can Do

Words and Music by
IRVING BERLIN

CHORUS
G7 C G7 C G7 C
1. Annie AN-Y-THING YOU CAN DO, I can do bet - ter, I can do an - y-thing bet-
2. Annie An-y-thing you can buy, I can buy cheap-er, I can buy an - y-thing cheap-
3. Annie An-y-one you can lick, I can lick fast - er, I can lick an - y - one fast-
mp-mf
G7 C G7 C
ter than you Frank No you can't Annie Yes I can Frank No you can't
er than you Frank Fif - ty cents Annie For - ty cents Frank Thir - ty cents
er than you Frank With your fist Annie With my feet Frank With your feet
G C G7 Dm7 G7
Annie Yes I can Frank No you can't Annie Yes I can Yes I can
Annie Twen-ty cents Frank No you can't Annie Yes I can Yes I can
Annie With an axe Frank No you can't Annie Yes I can Yes I can
G7 C G7 C G7 C
An-y-thing you can be, I can be great - er soon-er or lat - er, I'm great-
An-y-thing you can dig, I can dig deep - er I can dig an - y-thing deep-
An-y school where you went, I could be mas - ter I could be mas - ter much fast-

G7 C G7 C
er than you Frank No you're not Annie Yes I am Frank No you're not
er than you Frank Thir - ty feet Annie For - ty feet Frank Fif - ty feet
er than you Frank Can you spell Annie No I can't Frank Can you add
G7 C G7 Dm7 G7 C
Annie Yes I am Frank No you're not Annie Yes I am, Yes I am
Annie Six - ty feet Frank No you can't Annie Yes I can, Yes I can
Annie No I can't Frank Can you teach Annie Yes I can, Yes I can
Em Em6 Dm Dm6
Frank I can shoot a par-tridge with a sin-gle car-tridge Annie I can get a spar-row with
Frank I can drink my li - quor fast - er than a flick - er Annie I can do it quick-er and
Frank I could be a rac - er quite a stee-ple chas-er Annie I can jump a hurd-le e -
D7 Am7 D7 Am7 D7
a bow and ar - row Frank I can do most an - y - thing Annie Can
get e - ven sick - er Frank I can live on bread and cheese Annie And
ven with my gird - le Frank I can o - pen an - y safe Annie With

G7
Dm7
G9
G7
C
(Spoken)
(Sung)
you bake a pie? Frank No Annie Neith - er can I
on - ly on that? Frank Yes Annie So can a rat
out be - ing caught? Frank Yes Annie That's what I thought
An-y thing you can sing I
An-y note you can reach, I
An-y note you can hold I
can sing loud - er
can go high - er
can hold long - er
I can sing an - y - thing loud - er than you Frank No you can't
I can sing an - y - thing high - er than you Frank No you can't
I can hold an - y note long - er than you Frank No you can't
Annie Yes I can Frank No you can't Annie Yes I can Frank No you can't
Annie Yes I can Frank No you can't Annie Yes I can Frank No you can't
Annie Yes I can Frank No you can't Annie Yes I can Frank No you can't
Annie Yes I can Yes I can.
Annie Yes I can Yes I can.
Annie Yes I can Yes I can.
1.2.
3.
Fmaj7

You Can't Get A Man With A Gun

CHORUS
not too fast
mp-mf
C7 F F7 F7aug. B♭ Fdim C C7
1. I'm quick on the trig-ger, with tar-gets not much big-ger than a
2. cool, brave and dar-ing to see a li-on glar-ing when I'm
F Dm Dm7 G7 Gm7 C7 Fmaj.7 F7
pin-point I'm num-ber one But my score with a fel-ler is
out with my Rem-ing-ton But a look from a mis-ter will
B♭ B♭m F Fdim Gm7
low-er than a cel-lar, Oh, YOU CAN'T GET A MAN WITH A GUN.
raise a fev-er blis-ter, Oh, YOU CAN'T GET A MAN WITH A GUN.
C9 C7 F F7 F7aug. B♭ Fdim C C7
When I'm with a pis-tol, I spark-le like a crys-tal. Yes, I
The gals with um-brel-lers, are al-ways out with fel-lers in the

F Dm Dm7 G7 Gm7 C7 Fmaj.7
shine like the morn - ing sun but I lose all my
rain or the blaz - ing sun but a man nev - er
F7 Bb Bbm F C7
lus - ter when with a bron - co bus - ter, Oh, YOU CAN'T GET A MAN WITH A
tri - fles with gals who car - ry ri - fles, Oh, YOU CAN'T GET A MAN WITH A
F Gm7 F F7 Bb F
GUN with a gu - un with a gu - un No, YOU
GUN with a gu - un with a gu - un No, YOU
Dm7 G9 Gm7 C7 F
CAN'T GET A MAN WITH A GUN. If I went to
CAN'T GET A MAN WITH A GUN. A man's love is

F7 F7aug. B♭ Fdim C C7 F Dm Dm7 G7
bat - tle with some-one's herd of cat - tle, You'd have steak when the job was
might - y, he'll e - ven buy a night - y for a gal who he thinks is
Gm7 C7 Fmaj.7 F7 B♭
done but if I shot the her - der they'd hol - ler blood - y
fun but they don't buy pa - jam - as for pis - tol pack - in'
Gm7 B♭m F C7 F F9 B♭ B♭m
mur - der and you can't get a hug from a mug with a slug, Oh, YOU
ma - mas and you can't shoot a male in the tail like a quail, Oh, YOU
F C7 1.F Gm7 C7 2.F E♭ F
CAN'T GET A MAN WITH A GUN. I'm
CAN'T GET A MAN WITH A GUN.

My Defenses Are Down

Words and Music by
IRVING BERLIN

Slowly
CHORUS
Dm7
Cm7
Bbmaj7
Cm7
Bbmaj7
MY DE - FEN - SES ARE DOWN, she's brok - en my re - sist - ance and I
a tempo
mp-mf
Gm7
C7
Cm7
F7 Ebdim
Gm
Eb
F7
don't know where I am. I went in - to the fight like a li - on but I
Bb
Bbdim
Cm7
F7
Dm7
Cm7
Bbmaj7
came out like a lamb. MY DE - FEN - SES ARE DOWN, she's
Cm7
Bbmaj7
Gm7
C7
Cm7
F7
Ebdim
got me where she wants me and I can't es - cape no - how. I could

Gm7
Eb
Cm
Cm7
B♮7
speak to my heart when it weak-ened, but my heart won't lis - ten
Bb
Gb
Db7
Gb
now. Like a tooth - less claw - less ti - ger, like an
Db7
Gb
Bb
or - gan grind - er's bear, like a knight with - out his
Gm7
C9
Cm7
F9
Dm7
Cm7
Bbmaj7
ar-mor, like Sam - son_with-out his hair. MY DE - FEN-SES ARE DOWN. I

Cm7
Bbmaj7
Eb
Cm
D7-5
Fm
G7
G7-5
might as well sur-ren-der for the bat-tle can't be won, but I
C7
Cdim
Bb
Bbdim
F7
Cm7
F9
must con-fess that I like it, so there's noth-ing to be
Bb
G7-5
C7
Cdim
Bb
Bbm
C7
done. Yes, I must con-fess that I like it be-ing
F7
F9
1. Bb
Gb7
F7
Dm7
2. Bb
Ab
Bb
mis-'ra-ble is gon-na be fun. MY DE- fun.

I Got The Sun In The Morning

Words and Music by
IRVING BERLIN

C A7 Dm7 G7 C7
healthy-y bal-ance on the cred-it side
CHORUS
C7-5 F
Medium Jump Tempo
Got no dia-mond, got no pearl, still I think I'm a
mp-mf
F7 Bb F Gm7 F
luck-y girl, I GOT THE SUN IN THE MORN-ING and the moon at night
Bb F Gm7 F C7-5 F C7-5 F
Got no man-sion, Got no yacht,

C7-5
F
F7
B♭
F
still I'm hap - py with what I've got, I GOT THE SUN IN THE MORN-ING and the
Gm7
F
B♭
F
Gm7
F
A7
moon at night
Sun- shine
Am7
D9
G7
gives me a love - ly day
Moon - light
Gm7
C9
C7-5
F
gives me the milk - y way
Got no check- books,

C7-5
F
C7-5
F
F7
got no banks, still I'd like to ex- press my thanks. I GOT THE
Bb
F
Gm7
F
Bb
F
SUN IN THE MORN-ING and the moon at night
Gm7
F
F7
Bb
F
Fdim
Gm7
And with the sun in the morn - ing and the moon in the even- ing, I'm
C7-9
F
1.
C7
2.
Gb7
F
all right.

There's No Business Like Show Business

Words and Music by
IRVING BERLIN

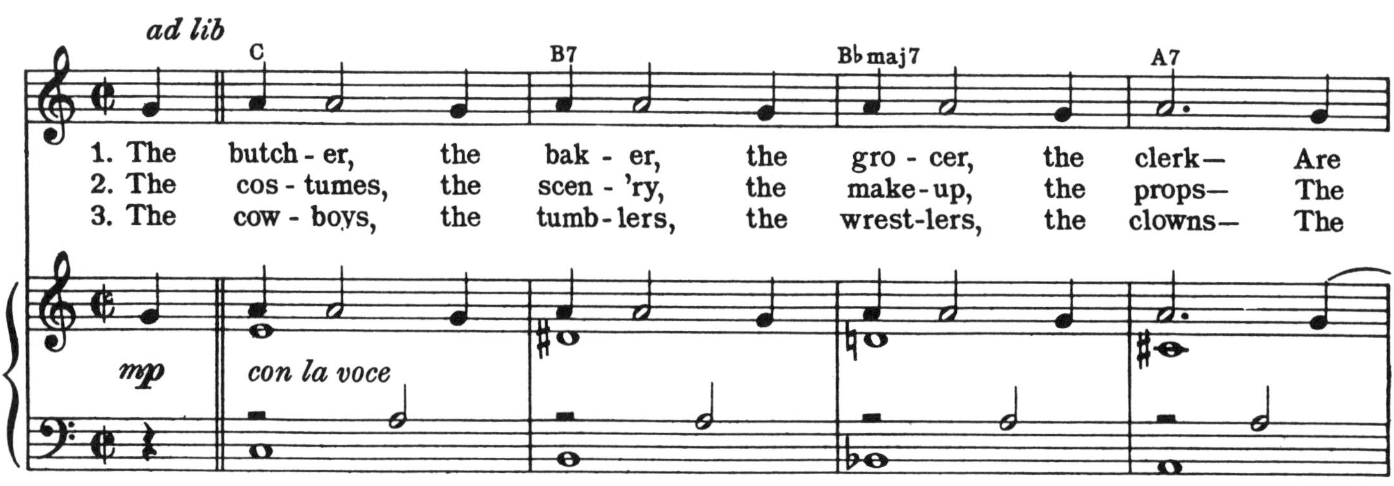

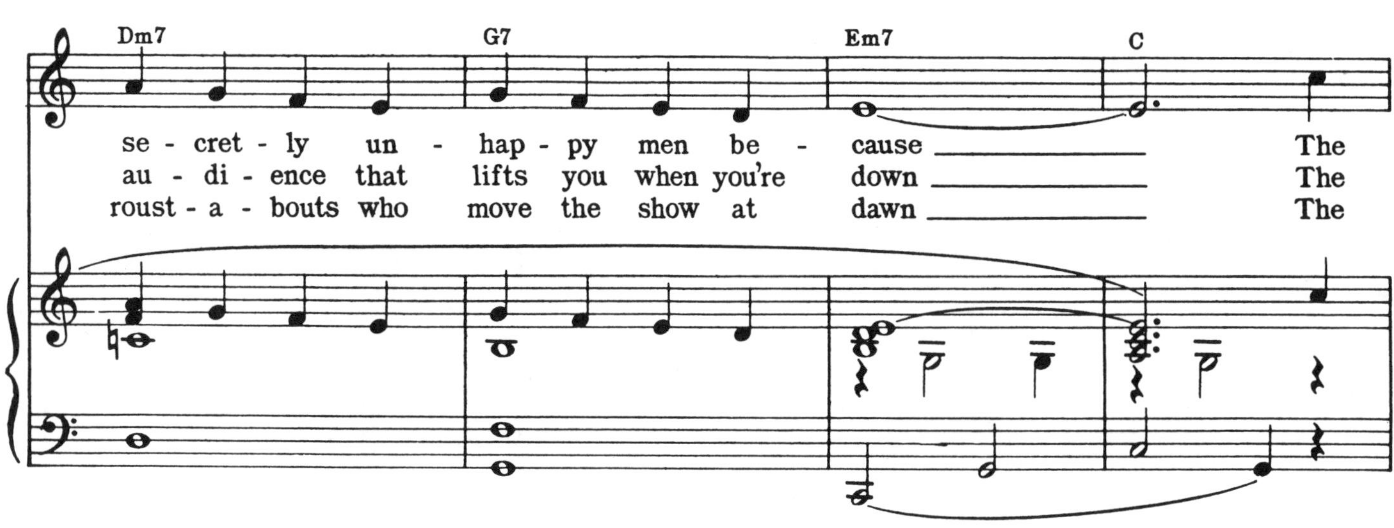

C9
Cdim
Fm
C
Cm
butch - er, the bak - er, the gro - cer, the clerk— Get
head - aches, the heart - aches, the back - aches, the flops— The
mu - sic, the spot - light, the peo - ple, the towns— Your
D7
G7
C
Dm7
C
paid for what they do but no ap - plause. They'd
sher - iff who es - corts you out of town. The
bag - gage with the lab - els pas - ted on. The
E
F#m7
B7
glad - ly bid their drear - y jobs good - bye. For
open - ing when your heart beats like a drum. The
saw - dust and the hor - ses and the smell. The
C
Dm7
G7
an - y - thing the - a - tri - cal and why.
clos - ing when the cus - tom - ers won't come.
towel you've tak - en from the last ho - tel.

CHORUS (brightly)
G7
C
THERE'S NO BUS - 'NESS LIKE SHOW BUS - 'NESS
1. like
2. like
3. like
a tempo
mp-mf
no bus - 'ness I know
no bus - 'ness I know
no bus - 'ness I know
Fm
Em7
C
G7
Dm7
G7
C
Ev - 'ry - thing a - bout it is ap - peal - ing.
You get word be - fore the show has start - ed.
Trav - 'ling thru the coun - try will be thrill - ing.
G7
Dm7
G7
C
Ev - 'ry - thing the traf - fic will al - low
That your fav - 'rite un - cle died at dawn
Stand - ing out in front on open - ing nights

G7
Dm7
G7
Am
Am7
No - where could you get that hap - py feel - ing, When you are
Top of that your Pa and Ma have part - ed, You're brok - en -
Smil - ing as you watch the thea - tre fill - ing, And there's your
Am7
D7
Dm7
G7
steal - ing that ex - tra bow There's
heart - ed but you go on There's
bill - ing out there in lights There's
C
no peo - ple like show peo - ple They
no peo - ple like show peo - ple They
no peo - ple like show peo - ple They
C7
Gm7
C7
Am7
F
smile when they are low
don't run out of dough
smile when they are low

Dm7 E7-5 A7
Ev - en with a tur - key that you know will fold You
An - gels come from ev - 'ry - where with lots of jack And
Yes - ter - day they told you you would not go far That
D7-5 G7 C A7
may be strand - ed out in the cold
when you lose it, there's no at - tack
night you o - pen and there you are
Dm7 E7-5 A7
Still you would - n't change it for a sack of gold
Where could you get mon - ey that you don't give back Let's
Next day on your dress - ing room they've hung a star
D7-5 G7
1. 2. C Em Dm7 G7
3. C Dm C
go on with the show. THERE'S show.

Moonshine Lullaby

Words and Music by
IRVING BERLIN

Dm7 G7 C Dm7 G7 Dm7 C
Bye, Bye Ba - by, Stop your yawn-ing
Dm7 G7 Ddim Am Am7 D7 G7
Don't cry Ba - by, Day will be dawn-ing
C G7 C G7 C Cdim
And when it does from the moun-tain where he wuz he'll be com-ing with a jug of
Dm7 G7 C C7 F Fm
moon - shine So count your sheep Mam-ma's sing - ing you to sleep With the

C
Cdim
Dm7
C
F
MOON - SHINE LULL-A - BY
Dream of Pap-py
C
Gm
A7
D7
G7
ver - y hap-py with his jug of moun-tain rye
C
C7
F
Fm
So count your sheep Mam - ma's sing - ing you to sleep with the
C
Cdim
Dm7
C
1.
Dm7
D♭9
2.
D♭7
C
MOON - SHINE LULL - A - BY.

Doin' What Comes Natur'lly

Words and Music by
IRVING BERLIN

C Cdim Dm7 G7 C Dm7
schools and books and learn - in' Still we've gone from A to Z
nev - er had a les - son Still she's learned to sing off key
G7 F G7 C G7 F G7 C
DO - IN' WHAT COMES NAT - UR - 'LLY (Kids) Do - in' what comes nat - ur - 'lly. You
DO - IN' WHAT COMES NAT - UR - 'LLY (Kids) Do - in' what comes nat - ur - 'lly. You
G7 C A7 Dm7 G7
don't have to know how to read or write when you're out with a fel - ler in the
don't have to go to a priv - ate school not to turn up your bus - tle to a
C G7 C A7
pale moon - light. You don't have to look in a book to find what he
stub - born mule. You don't have to have a pro - fess - or's dome not to

Dm7 G7 C Dm7 G7
thinks of the moon and what is on his mind. That comes
go for the hon - ey when the bee's at home. That comes
C Dm7 G7 C E F#m7 B7
nat - ur - 'lly (Kids) That comes nat - ur - 'lly. My un - cle out in
nat - ur - 'lly (Kids) That comes nat - ur - 'lly. My ti - ny ba - by
mp
E F#m7 B7 E
Tex - as can't e - ven write his name, he
broth - er who's nev - er read a book, knows
F#m7 B7 E Cm D7 G7
signs his checks with "x' - s," but they cash them just the same.
one sex from the oth - er, all he had to do was look.

C
Dm7
C
Cdim
If you saw my Paw and Maw you'd know they had no
Grand - paw Bill lives on the hill with some - one he just
Dm7
G7
C
Dm7
G7
F
G7
learn - in', Still they raised a fam - il - y DO - IN' WHAT COMES
mar - ried, There he is at nine - ty - three DO - IN' WHAT COMES
1.
C
G7
F
G7
C
NAT - UR - 'LLY (Kids) Do - in' what comes nat - ur - 'lly.
NAT - UR - 'LLY
2.
G7
F
G7
C
G7
F
G7
C
(Kids) Do - in' what comes nat - ur - 'lly.

The Girl That I Marry

Words and Music by
IRVING BERLIN

F7
B♭
C7
F7
girl I call my own will wear
B♭
Cm
B♭
F7
sat - ins and lac - es and smell of col - ogne. Her
B♭
Cm7
F7
nails will be pol - ished and in her hair, she'll wear a gar -
B♭
B♭9
den - ia, and I'll be there 'stead of flit - tin' I'll be

E♭
B♭dim
sit - tin' Next to her and she'll purr like a
B♭ Fdim F7 Dm F9 B♭ Fdim F7 Cm7
kit - ten A doll I can car - ry the girl that I
(kit - tin)
F7 Cm7 F7
1.
B♭ Cm7 F7 B♭
mar - ry must be.
THE
2.
B♭ Cm7 F7 B♭
be.

They Say It's Wonderful

Words and Music by
IRVING BERLIN

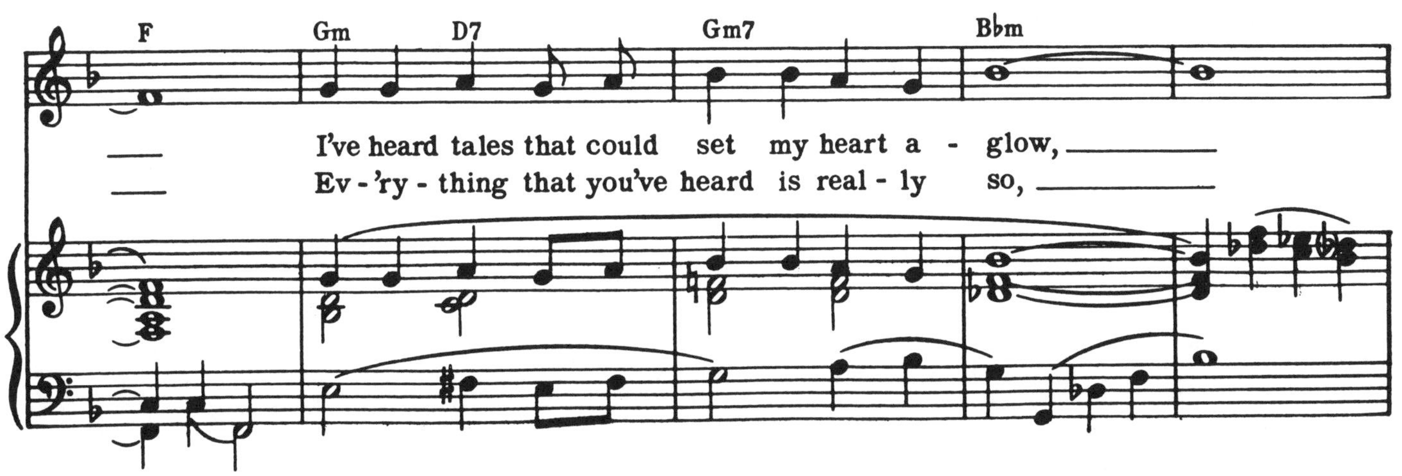

F Dm7 Gm7 G♭7 F D♭9
Wish I knew if the things I hear are so.
I've been there once or twice and I should know.
accel.
rall.
CHORUS
Gm7 B♭m6 C7 F Fdim
(Annie) 1. They say that fall-ing in love is won-der-ful it's
(Frank) 2. You'll find that fall-ing in love is won-der-ful it's
a tempo
mp-mf
B♭m C7-9 C7 Am7 F D9 Cdim Gm B♭m6 C7
won-der-ful so they say And with a moon up a-bove, it's
won-der-ful (Annie) so you say (Frank) And with a moon up a-bove, it's
F Fdim B♭m C7-9 C7 F7 F9-5 F9
won-der-ful it's won-der-ful so they tell me.
won-der-ful it's won-der-ful (Annie) so you tell me.

F7aug Bb Bbm F Am Fdim
I can't re-call who said it, I know I nev-er read it. I
(Frank) To leave your house some morn-ing, and with-out an-y warn-ing, you're
Am Fdim Am Db9 Gm7
on-ly know they tell me that love is grand and the thing that's
stop-ping peo-ple shout-ing that love is grand and to hold a
Bbm6 C7 Am7 D7aug-9 D7 Dm7 G9 Gm7
known as ro-mance is won-der-ful, won-der-ful in ev-'ry way
man in your arms is won-der-ful, won-der-ful in ev-'ry way
C7-5 F Gm7 F Db9 F Dm7 Gm7 Gb7 F
so they say
(Annie) so you say
rall.

An Old Fashioned Wedding

Words and Music by
IRVING BERLIN

F Fdim C7 F C7 F Gm7 F F+ F Fdim C7 F F7
Some-where in some lit - tle chap-el, Some - day when or-ange blos-soms
Bb maj7 Bb+ Bb6 Gm Gm (maj7) Gm7 C7 F
bloom, We'll have AN OLD FASH-IONED WED-DING,
F#dim Gm7 C7 Gm7 C7 F F6 Fmaj7 F6
A sim-ple wed-ding for an old fash-ioned bride and groom.
2nd CHORUS: with a lift
F F6 Fmaj7 F6 F F6 Fmaj7 F6
I wan-na wed-ding in a big church with brides - maids and flow-er girls,
F F6 Fmaj7 F6 Gm Gm6 Gm7 C7
A lot of ush-ers in tail - coats, re - port-ers and pho - to-graph - ers.

Gm Gm(maj7) B♭m F G7 C7 B♭m6 C7
A cer-e-mo-ny by a bish-op who will tie the knot and say: "Do you a-gree to love and
F Dm Dm7 G7 Gm7 C7 F F6 Fmaj7 F6
hon-or," Love and hon-or, yes, but not o - bey. I wan-na wed-ding ring sur-round - ed by
F F6 Fmaj7 F6 F F6 Fmaj7 F6 Gm Gm6
dia - monds in plat-i - num, A big re-cep-tion at the Wal - dorf with cham - pagne and
Gm7 C7 Gm Gm(maj7) B♭m F G7 C7 Gm7 C7
cav-i - ar. I wan-na wed-ding like the Van-der-bilts have, ev-'ry-thing big, not small. If I
F Gm Am F G7 C7 F F6 Fmaj7 F6
can't have that kind of a wed-ding I don't wan-na get mar-ried at all.

3rd CHORUS: (DUET)
with expression
F
F6
F
F6
Fmaj7
F6
We'll have AN OLD - FASH-IONED WED-DING,
with a lift
I wan-na wed-ding in a big church with brides - maids and flow-er girls,
mp
F
F6
Gm
Gm6
Gm7
C7
Blessed in the good old fash-ioned way.
A lot of ush-ers in tail - coats, re - port-ers and pho - to-graph-ers,
Gm
Gm(maj7)
B♭m
Gm7
C7
G9
C9
Gm7
I'll vow to love you for - ev - er,
You'll vow to
A cer-e-mo-ny by a bish-op who will tie the knot and say:

Gm7 C9 F Gm7 C7
love and hon - or and o - bey.
"Do you a-gree to love and hon-or," Love and hon-or, yes, but not o - bey.
F F6 F F6 Fmaj7 F6
Some - where in some lit - tle chap - el,
I wan-na wed-ding ring sur-round - ed by dia - monds in plat - i - num,
F F6 F7 B♭ B♭6
Some - day when or - ange blos-soms bloom.
A big re-cep-tion at the Wal - dorf with cham - pagne and cav - i - ar.

Gm7
C9
F
We'll have AN OLD FASH-IONED WED-DING, A sim-ple
I wan-na wed-ding like the Van-der-bilts have, ev - 'ry-thing big, not small. If I
Gm7
C7
F
wed-ding for an old fash-ioned bride and groom
can't have that kind of a wed - ding I don't wan-na get mar-ried at all
Gm7
C7
F
We'll have AN OLD FASH-IONED WED-DING.
If it's not a big wed-ding I don't wan-na get mar-ried at all.

I'll Share It All With You

Words and Music by
IRVING BERLIN

Cm7 Dm7 Cm7 B♭dim B♭
Cm7
F7
B♭7
B♭dim Fm7 B♭7+(♭9)
— For-tune's door shut, can't get in, but just the same
CHORUS
Medium Jump Tempo
E♭7
D7
D♭7
C7
My ear for mus - ic, my feet for danc ing,
Winnie: My head for think - ing, my face for smil - ing,
mp-mf
F7(♭5)
B♭7
E♭
B♭9
E♭
Fm7 B♭7
my lips for kiss - ing, I'LL SHARE IT ALL WITH YOU.
my hands for cook - ing, I'LL SHARE IT ALL WITH YOU.

Eb7
D7
Db7
C7
F7(b5)
My sense of hum - or, my dis-po - si - tion, my
My un-der-stand - ing, my lov-ing na - ture, my
Bb7
Eb
Bb9
Eb
Fm7
Bb7
ros-y fu - ture, I'LL SHARE IT ALL WITH YOU.
good in - ten - tions, I'LL SHARE IT ALL WITH YOU.
Some day hon - ey
I'm not twen - ty
Eb
Fm7
Bb7aug
Eb
Cm
D7
I'll have mon - ey, you know what that brings, furs and dia - mond rings
But there's plen - ty un - der - neath my hat, I know where I'm at

Gm
D7
B♭7
B♭7aug
E♭7
and be - sides those things there'll be my
and on top of that there'll be my
D7
D♭7
C7
F7(♭5)
ear for mus - ic, my feet for danc - ing, my
ear for mus - ic, my feet for danc - ing, my
B♭7
E♭
Fm7
E♮maj7
E♭
1.
Fm7
B♭7aug
2.
E♭7
E♭
lips for kiss - ing, I'LL SHARE IT ALL WITH YOU.
lips for kiss - ing, I'LL SHARE IT ALL WITH YOU.

I Got Lost In His Arms

Words and Music by
IRVING BERLIN

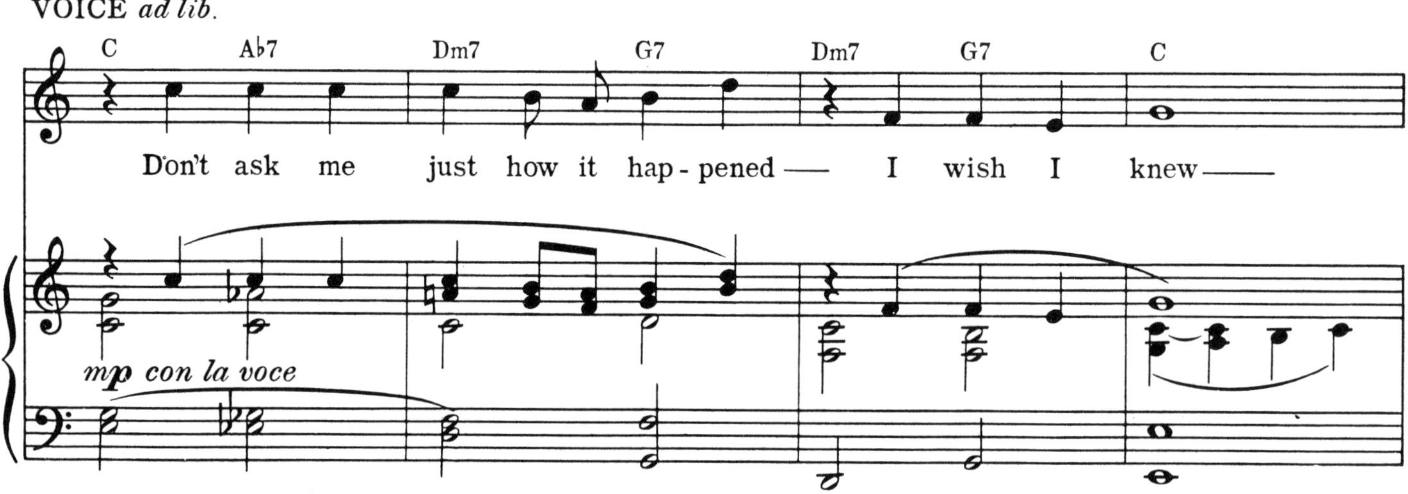

CHORUS
G7 G7aug Em7 C Cmaj7 C6 A7aug
I GOT LOST IN HIS ARMS and I had to stay — It was
a tempo
mp mf
Fmaj7 Dm Dm7 D♭7 C7 Gm7
dark in his arms and I lost my way — From the dark came a
D9 Fm7 C Dm7 G7 Gdim
voice and it seemed to say — "There you go — There you
Dm7 Fm G7 G7aug Em7 C Cmaj7 C6
go" — How I felt as I fell I just can't re - call —

A7aug Fmaj7 Dm Dm7 D♭7 C7
But his arms held me fast and it broke the fall and I
Gm7 Fmaj7 Fm C Cdim
said to my heart as it fool-ish-ly kept jump-ing all a-
Dm7 G7 B♭m B♭dim Dm7 G7 Dm7 Fm C
round I got lost but look what I found.
rall.
1. Em7 Dm7 G7 G7aug
I GOT
a tempo
2. C F C
pp